The Comedy of Errors

William Shakespeare

Akasha Publishing

Akasha Classic Series

Akasha Classics is dedicated to the re-publication of cherished works of World Literature. Many of these writings play a special role in recording the history of human kind, who we are and where we have been.

Akasha Publishing, LLC
877-745-7317
AkashaPublishing.Com

The Comedy of Errors, by William Shakespeare

Library of Congress Control Number: 2009912204

ISBN-13: 978-1-60512-552-7   Hardcover
ISBN-13: 978-1-60512-590-9   Paperback

Shakespeare Titles

Title	Hardcover ISBN	Paperback ISBN
A Midsummer Night's Dream	978-1-60512-544-2	978-1-60512-582-4
All's Well That Ends Well	978-1-60512-545-9	978-1-60512-583-1
Antony and Cleopatra	978-1-60512-572-5	978-1-60512-610-4
As You Like It	978-1-60512-546-6	978-1-60512-584-8
Coriolanus	978-1-60512-573-2	978-1-60512-611-1
Cymbeline	978-1-60512-547-3	978-1-60512-585-5
Hamlet, Prince of Denmark	978-1-60512-574-9	978-1-60512-612-8
Julius Caesar	978-1-60512-575-6	978-1-60512-613-5
King Henry IV, Part 1	978-1-60512-562-6	978-1-60512-600-5
King Henry IV, Part 2	978-1-60512-563-3	978-1-60512-601-2
King Henry V	978-1-60512-564-0	978-1-60512-602-9
King Henry VI, Part 1	978-1-60512-565-7	978-1-60512-603-6
King Henry VI, Part 2	978-1-60512-566-4	978-1-60512-604-3
King Henry VI, Part 3	978-1-60512-567-1	978-1-60512-605-0
King Henry VIII	978-1-60512-568-8	978-1-60512-606-7
King John	978-1-60512-569-5	978-1-60512-607-4
King Lear	978-1-60512-576-3	978-1-60512-614-2
King Richard II	978-1-60512-570-1	978-1-60512-608-1
King Richard III	978-1-60512-571-8	978-1-60512-609-8
Loves Labours Lost	978-1-60512-548-0	978-1-60512-586-2
Macbeth	978-1-60512-577-0	978-1-60512-615-9
Measure for Measure	978-1-60512-549-7	978-1-60512-587-9
Much Ado About Nothing	978-1-60512-550-3	978-1-60512-588-6
Othello, the Moore of Venice	978-1-60512-578-7	978-1-60512-616-6
Pericles, Prince of Tyre	978-1-60512-551-0	978-1-60512-589-3
Romeo and Juliet	978-1-60512-579-4	978-1-60512-617-3
The Comedy of Errors	978-1-60512-552-7	978-1-60512-590-9
The Merchant of Venice	978-1-60512-553-4	978-1-60512-591-6
The Merry Wives of Windsor	978-1-60512-554-1	978-1-60512-592-3
The Sonnets and other Poems	978-1-60512-561-9	978-1-60512-599-2
The Taming of the Shrew	978-1-60512-555-8	978-1-60512-593-0
The Tempest	978-1-60512-556-5	978-1-60512-594-7
Timon of Athens	978-1-60512-580-0	978-1-60512-618-0
Titus Andronicus	978-1-60512-581-7	978-1-60512-619-7
Troilus and Cressida	978-1-60512-557-2	978-1-60512-595-4
Twelfth Night	978-1-60512-558-9	978-1-60512-596-1
Two Gentlemen of Verona	978-1-60512-559-6	978-1-60512-597-8
Winter's Tale	978-1-60512-560-2	978-1-60512-598-5

William Shakespeare
(baptised 26 April 1564 – died 23 April 1616)

William Shakespeare was an English poet and playwright, widely regarded as the greatest writer in the English language and the world's preeminent dramatist. He is often called England's national poet and the "Bard of Avon". His surviving works, including some collaborations, consist of 38 plays, 154 sonnets, two long narrative poems, and several other poems. His plays have been translated into every major living language and are performed more often than those of any other playwright.

Shakespeare was born and raised in Stratford-upon-Avon. At the age of 18, he married Anne Hathaway, who bore him three children: Susanna, and twins Hamnet and Judith. Between 1585 and 1592, he began a successful career in London as an actor, writer, and part owner of a playing company called the Lord Chamberlain's Men, later known as the King's Men. He appears to have retired to Stratford around 1613, where he died three years later. Few records of Shakespeare's private life survive, and there has been considerable speculation about such matters as his physical appearance, sexuality, religious beliefs, and whether the works attributed to him were written by others.

Shakespeare produced most of his known work between 1589 and 1613. His early plays were mainly comedies and histories, genres he raised to the peak of sophistication and artistry by the end of the sixteenth century. He then wrote mainly tragedies until about 1608, including Hamlet, King Lear, and Macbeth, considered some of the finest works in the English language. In his last phase, he wrote tragicomedies, also known as romances, and collaborated with other playwrights.

The Comedy of Errors

By William Shakespeare

Dramatis Personae

SOLINUS Duke of Ephesus. (DUKE SOLINUS:)
AEGEON a merchant of Syracuse.
ANTIPHOLUS OF EPHESUS, ANTIPHOLUS OF
SYRACUSE } twin brothers, and sons to AEgeon and
AEmilia.
DROMIO OF EPHESUS, DROMIO OF SYRACUSE }
twin brothers, and attendants on the two
Antipholuses.
BALTHAZAR a merchant
ANGELO a goldsmith.
First Merchant friend to Antipholus of Syracuse.
Second Merchant to whom Angelo is a debtor.
PINCH a schoolmaster.
AEMILIA wife to AEgeon, an abbess at Ephesus.
ADRIANA wife to Antipholus of Ephesus.
LUCIANA her sister.
LUCE servant to Adriana.
A Courtezan.
Gaoler, Officers, and other Attendants

[*Scene: Ephesus.*]

The Comedy of Errors

By William Shakespeare

ACT I

SCENE I. A hall in DUKE SOLINUS'S palace.

Enter DUKE SOLINUS, AEGEON, Gaoler, Officers, and
other Attendants

AEGEON
Proceed, Solinus, to procure my fall
And by the doom of death end woes and all.

DUKE SOLINUS
Merchant of Syracuse, plead no more;
I am not partial to infringe our laws:
The enmity and discord which of late
Sprung from the rancorous outrage of your duke
To merchants, our well-dealing countrymen,
Who wanting guilders to redeem their lives
Have seal'd his rigorous statutes with their bloods,
Excludes all pity from our threatening looks.
For, since the mortal and intestine jars
'Twixt thy seditious countrymen and us,
It hath in solemn synods been decreed
Both by the Syracusians and ourselves,
To admit no traffic to our adverse towns Nay, more,
If any born at Ephesus be seen
At any Syracusian marts and fairs;
Again: if any Syracusian born
Come to the bay of Ephesus, he dies,
His goods confiscate to the duke's dispose,
Unless a thousand marks be levied,
To quit the penalty and to ransom him.
Thy substance, valued at the highest rate,
Cannot amount unto a hundred marks;
Therefore by law thou art condemned to die.

AEGEON
Yet this my comfort: when your words are done,

My woes end likewise with the evening sun.

DUKE SOLINUS
Well, Syracusian, say in brief the cause
Why thou departed'st from thy native home
And for what cause thou camest to Ephesus.

AEGEON
A heavier task could not have been imposed
Than I to speak my griefs unspeakable:
Yet, that the world may witness that my end
Was wrought by nature, not by vile offence,
I'll utter what my sorrows give me leave.
In Syracusa was I born, and wed
Unto a woman, happy but for me,
And by me, had not our hap been bad.
With her I lived in joy; our wealth increased
By prosperous voyages I often made
To Epidamnum; till my factor's death
And the great care of goods at random left
Drew me from kind embracements of my spouse:
From whom my absence was not six months old
Before herself, almost at fainting under
The pleasing punishment that women bear,
Had made provision for her following me
And soon and safe arrived where I was.
There had she not been long, but she became
A joyful mother of two goodly sons;
And, which was strange, the one so like the other,
As could not be distinguish'd but by names.
That very hour, and in the self-same inn,
A meaner woman was delivered
Of such a burden, male twins, both alike:
Those,--for their parents were exceeding poor,--
I bought and brought up to attend my sons.
My wife, not meanly proud of two such boys,
Made daily motions for our home return:
Unwilling I agreed. Alas! too soon,
We came aboard.

A league from Epidamnum had we sail'd,
Before the always wind-obeying deep
Gave any tragic instance of our harm:
But longer did we not retain much hope;
For what obscured light the heavens did grant
Did but convey unto our fearful minds
A doubtful warrant of immediate death;
Which though myself would gladly have embraced,
Yet the incessant weepings of my wife,
Weeping before for what she saw must come,
And piteous plainings of the pretty babes,
That mourn'd for fashion, ignorant what to fear,
Forced me to seek delays for them and me.
And this it was, for other means was none:
The sailors sought for safety by our boat,
And left the ship, then sinking-ripe, to us:
My wife, more careful for the latter-born,
Had fasten'd him unto a small spare mast,
Such as seafaring men provide for storms;
To him one of the other twins was bound,
Whilst I had been like heedful of the other:
The children thus disposed, my wife and I,
Fixing our eyes on whom our care was fix'd,
Fasten'd ourselves at either end the mast;
And floating straight, obedient to the stream,
Was carried towards Corinth, as we thought.
At length the sun, gazing upon the earth,
Dispersed those vapours that offended us;
And by the benefit of his wished light,
The seas wax'd calm, and we discovered
Two ships from far making amain to us,
Of Corinth that, of Epidaurus this:
But ere they came,--O, let me say no more!
Gather the sequel by that went before.

DUKE SOLINUS
Nay, forward, old man; do not break off so;
For we may pity, though not pardon thee.

AEGEON

O, had the gods done so, I had not now
Worthily term'd them merciless to us!
For, ere the ships could meet by twice five leagues,
We were encounterd by a mighty rock;
Which being violently borne upon,
Our helpful ship was splitted in the midst;
So that, in this unjust divorce of us,
Fortune had left to both of us alike
What to delight in, what to sorrow for.
Her part, poor soul! seeming as burdened
With lesser weight but not with lesser woe,
Was carried with more speed before the wind;
And in our sight they three were taken up
By fishermen of Corinth, as we thought.
At length, another ship had seized on us;
And, knowing whom it was their hap to save,
Gave healthful welcome to their shipwreck'd guests;
And would have reft the fishers of their prey,
Had not their bark been very slow of sail;
And therefore homeward did they bend their course.
Thus have you heard me sever'd from my bliss;
That by misfortunes was my life prolong'd,
To tell sad stories of my own mishaps.

DUKE SOLINUS

And for the sake of them thou sorrowest for,
Do me the favour to dilate at full
What hath befall'n of them and thee till now.

AEGEON

My youngest boy, and yet my eldest care,
At eighteen years became inquisitive
After his brother: and importuned me
That his attendant--so his case was like,
Reft of his brother, but retain'd his name--
Might bear him company in the quest of him:
Whom whilst I labour'd of a love to see,

I hazarded the loss of whom I loved.
Five summers have I spent in furthest Greece,
Roaming clean through the bounds of Asia,
And, coasting homeward, came to Ephesus;
Hopeless to find, yet loath to leave unsought
Or that or any place that harbours men.
But here must end the story of my life;
And happy were I in my timely death,
Could all my travels warrant me they live.

DUKE SOLINUS
Hapless AEgeon, whom the fates have mark'd
To bear the extremity of dire mishap!
Now, trust me, were it not against our laws,
Against my crown, my oath, my dignity,
Which princes, would they, may not disannul,
My soul would sue as advocate for thee.
But, though thou art adjudged to the death
And passed sentence may not be recall'd
But to our honour's great disparagement,
Yet I will favour thee in what I can.
Therefore, merchant, I'll limit thee this day
To seek thy life by beneficial help:
Try all the friends thou hast in Ephesus;
Beg thou, or borrow, to make up the sum,
And live; if no, then thou art doom'd to die.
Gaoler, take him to thy custody.

Gaoler
I will, my lord.

AEGEON
Hopeless and helpless doth AEgeon wend,
But to procrastinate his lifeless end.

Exeunt

SCENE II. The Mart.

Enter ANTIPHOLUS of Syracuse, DROMIO of
Syracuse, and First Merchant

First Merchant
Therefore give out you are of Epidamnum,
Lest that your goods too soon be confiscate.
This very day a Syracusian merchant
Is apprehended for arrival here;
And not being able to buy out his life
According to the statute of the town,
Dies ere the weary sun set in the west.
There is your money that I had to keep.

ANTIPHOLUS OF SYRACUSE
Go bear it to the Centaur, where we host,
And stay there, Dromio, till I come to thee.
Within this hour it will be dinner-time:
Till that, I'll view the manners of the town,
Peruse the traders, gaze upon the buildings,
And then return and sleep within mine inn,
For with long travel I am stiff and weary.
Get thee away.

DROMIO OF SYRACUSE
Many a man would take you at your word,
And go indeed, having so good a mean.

Exit

ANTIPHOLUS OF SYRACUSE
A trusty villain, sir, that very oft,
When I am dull with care and melancholy,
Lightens my humour with his merry jests.
What, will you walk with me about the town,
And then go to my inn and dine with me?

First Merchant
I am invited, sir, to certain merchants,
Of whom I hope to make much benefit;
I crave your pardon. Soon at five o'clock,
Please you, I'll meet with you upon the mart
And afterward consort you till bed-time:
My present business calls me from you now.

ANTIPHOLUS OF SYRACUSE
Farewell till then: I will go lose myself
And wander up and down to view the city.

First Merchant
Sir, I commend you to your own content.

Exit

ANTIPHOLUS OF SYRACUSE
He that commends me to mine own content
Commends me to the thing I cannot get.
I to the world am like a drop of water
That in the ocean seeks another drop,
Who, falling there to find his fellow forth,
Unseen, inquisitive, confounds himself:
So I, to find a mother and a brother,
In quest of them, unhappy, lose myself.

Enter DROMIO of Ephesus

Here comes the almanac of my true date.
What now? how chance thou art return'd so soon?

DROMIO OF EPHESUS
Return'd so soon! rather approach'd too late:
The capon burns, the pig falls from the spit,
The clock hath strucken twelve upon the bell;
My mistress made it one upon my cheek:
She is so hot because the meat is cold;

The meat is cold because you come not home;
You come not home because you have no stomach;
You have no stomach having broke your fast;
But we that know what 'tis to fast and pray
Are penitent for your default to-day.

ANTIPHOLUS OF SYRACUSE
Stop in your wind, sir: tell me this, I pray:
Where have you left the money that I gave you?

DROMIO OF EPHESUS
O,--sixpence, that I had o' Wednesday last
To pay the saddler for my mistress' crupper?
The saddler had it, sir; I kept it not.

ANTIPHOLUS OF SYRACUSE
I am not in a sportive humour now:
Tell me, and dally not, where is the money?
We being strangers here, how darest thou trust
So great a charge from thine own custody?

DROMIO OF EPHESUS
I pray you, air, as you sit at dinner:
I from my mistress come to you in post;
If I return, I shall be post indeed,
For she will score your fault upon my pate.
Methinks your maw, like mine, should be your clock,
And strike you home without a messenger.

ANTIPHOLUS OF SYRACUSE
Come, Dromio, come, these jests are out of season;
Reserve them till a merrier hour than this.
Where is the gold I gave in charge to thee?

DROMIO OF EPHESUS
To me, sir? why, you gave no gold to me.

ANTIPHOLUS OF SYRACUSE
Come on, sir knave, have done your foolishness,

And tell me how thou hast disposed thy charge.

DROMIO OF EPHESUS
My charge was but to fetch you from the mart
Home to your house, the Phoenix, sir, to dinner:
My mistress and her sister stays for you.

ANTIPHOLUS OF SYRACUSE
In what safe place you have bestow'd my money,
Or I shall break that merry sconce of yours
That stands on tricks when I am undisposed:
Where is the thousand marks thou hadst of me?

DROMIO OF EPHESUS
I have some marks of yours upon my pate,
Some of my mistress' marks upon my shoulders,
But not a thousand marks between you both.
If I should pay your worship those again,
Perchance you will not bear them patiently.

ANTIPHOLUS OF SYRACUSE
Thy mistress' marks? what mistress, slave, hast thou?

DROMIO OF EPHESUS
Your worship's wife, my mistress at the Phoenix;
She that doth fast till you come home to dinner,
And prays that you will hie you home to dinner.

ANTIPHOLUS OF SYRACUSE
What, wilt thou flout me thus unto my face,
Being forbid? There, take you that, sir knave.

DROMIO OF EPHESUS
What mean you, sir? for God's sake, hold your hands!
Nay, and you will not, sir, I'll take my heels.

Exit

ANTIPHOLUS OF SYRACUSE
Upon my life, by some device or other
The villain is o'er-raught of all my money.
They say this town is full of cozenage,
As, nimble jugglers that deceive the eye,
Dark-working sorcerers that change the mind,
Soul-killing witches that deform the body,
Disguised cheaters, prating mountebanks,
And many such-like liberties of sin:
If it prove so, I will be gone the sooner.
I'll to the Centaur, to go seek this slave:
I greatly fear my money is not safe.

Exit

ACT II

SCENE I. The house of ANTIPHOLUS of Ephesus.

Enter ADRIANA and LUCIANA

ADRIANA
Neither my husband nor the slave return'd,
That in such haste I sent to seek his master!
Sure, Luciana, it is two o'clock.

LUCIANA
Perhaps some merchant hath invited him,
And from the mart he's somewhere gone to dinner.
Good sister, let us dine and never fret:
A man is master of his liberty:
Time is their master, and, when they see time,
They'll go or come: if so, be patient, sister.

ADRIANA
Why should their liberty than ours be more?

LUCIANA
Because their business still lies out o' door.

ADRIANA
Look, when I serve him so, he takes it ill.

LUCIANA
O, know he is the bridle of your will.

ADRIANA
There's none but asses will be bridled so.

LUCIANA
Why, headstrong liberty is lash'd with woe.
There's nothing situate under heaven's eye
But hath his bound, in earth, in sea, in sky:

The beasts, the fishes, and the winged fowls,
Are their males' subjects and at their controls:
Men, more divine, the masters of all these,
Lords of the wide world and wild watery seas,
Indued with intellectual sense and souls,
Of more preeminence than fish and fowls,
Are masters to their females, and their lords:
Then let your will attend on their accords.

ADRIANA
This servitude makes you to keep unwed.

LUCIANA
Not this, but troubles of the marriage-bed.

ADRIANA
But, were you wedded, you would bear some sway.

LUCIANA
Ere I learn love, I'll practise to obey.

ADRIANA
How if your husband start some other where?

LUCIANA
Till he come home again, I would forbear.

ADRIANA
Patience unmoved! no marvel though she pause;
They can be meek that have no other cause.
A wretched soul, bruised with adversity,
We bid be quiet when we hear it cry;
But were we burdened with like weight of pain,
As much or more would we ourselves complain:
So thou, that hast no unkind mate to grieve thee,
With urging helpless patience wouldst relieve me,
But, if thou live to see like right bereft,
This fool-begg'd patience in thee will be left.

LUCIANA
Well, I will marry one day, but to try.
Here comes your man; now is your husband nigh.

Enter DROMIO of Ephesus

ADRIANA
Say, is your tardy master now at hand?

DROMIO OF EPHESUS
Nay, he's at two hands with me, and that my two ears
can witness.

ADRIANA
Say, didst thou speak with him? know'st thou his
mind?

DROMIO OF EPHESUS
Ay, ay, he told his mind upon mine ear:
Beshrew his hand, I scarce could understand it.

LUCIANA
Spake he so doubtfully, thou couldst not feel his
meaning?

DROMIO OF EPHESUS
Nay, he struck so plainly, I could too well feel his
blows; and withal so doubtfully that I could scarce
understand them.

ADRIANA
But say, I prithee, is he coming home? It seems he
hath great care to please his wife.

DROMIO OF EPHESUS
Why, mistress, sure my master is horn-mad.

ADRIANA
Horn-mad, thou villain!

DROMIO OF EPHESUS
I mean not cuckold-mad;
But, sure, he is stark mad.
When I desired him to come home to dinner,
He ask'd me for a thousand marks in gold:
''Tis dinner-time,' quoth I; 'My gold!' quoth he;
'Your meat doth burn,' quoth I; 'My gold!' quoth he:
'Will you come home?' quoth I; 'My gold!' quoth he.
'Where is the thousand marks I gave thee, villain?'
'The pig,' quoth I, 'is burn'd;' 'My gold!' quoth he:
'My mistress, sir' quoth I; 'Hang up thy mistress!
I know not thy mistress; out on thy mistress!'

LUCIANA
Quoth who?

DROMIO OF EPHESUS
Quoth my master:
'I know,' quoth he, 'no house, no wife, no mistress.'
So that my errand, due unto my tongue,
I thank him, I bare home upon my shoulders;
For, in conclusion, he did beat me there.

ADRIANA
Go back again, thou slave, and fetch him home.

DROMIO OF EPHESUS
Go back again, and be new beaten home?
For God's sake, send some other messenger.

ADRIANA
Back, slave, or I will break thy pate across.

DROMIO OF EPHESUS
And he will bless that cross with other beating:
Between you I shall have a holy head.

ADRIANA
Hence, prating peasant! fetch thy master home.

DROMIO OF EPHESUS
Am I so round with you as you with me,
That like a football you do spurn me thus?
You spurn me hence, and he will spurn me hither:
If I last in this service, you must case me in leather.

Exit

LUCIANA
Fie, how impatience loureth in your face!

ADRIANA
His company must do his minions grace,
Whilst I at home starve for a merry look.
Hath homely age the alluring beauty took
From my poor cheek? then he hath wasted it:
Are my discourses dull? barren my wit?
If voluble and sharp discourse be marr'd,
Unkindness blunts it more than marble hard:
Do their gay vestments his affections bait?
That's not my fault: he's master of my state:
What ruins are in me that can be found,
By him not ruin'd? then is he the ground
Of my defeatures. My decayed fair
A sunny look of his would soon repair
But, too unruly deer, he breaks the pale
And feeds from home; poor I am but his stale.

LUCIANA
Self-harming jealousy! fie, beat it hence!

ADRIANA
Unfeeling fools can with such wrongs dispense.
I know his eye doth homage otherwhere,
Or else what lets it but he would be here?
Sister, you know he promised me a chain;

Would that alone, alone he would detain,
So he would keep fair quarter with his bed!
I see the jewel best enamelled
Will lose his beauty; yet the gold bides still,
That others touch, and often touching will
Wear gold: and no man that hath a name,
By falsehood and corruption doth it shame.
Since that my beauty cannot please his eye,
I'll weep what's left away, and weeping die.

LUCIANA
How many fond fools serve mad jealousy!

Exeunt

SCENE II. A public place.

Enter ANTIPHOLUS of Syracuse

ANTIPHOLUS OF SYRACUSE
The gold I gave to Dromio is laid up
Safe at the Centaur; and the heedful slave
Is wander'd forth, in care to seek me out
By computation and mine host's report.
I could not speak with Dromio since at first
I sent him from the mart. See, here he comes.

Enter DROMIO of Syracuse

How now sir! is your merry humour alter'd?
As you love strokes, so jest with me again.
You know no Centaur? you received no gold?
Your mistress sent to have me home to dinner?
My house was at the Phoenix? Wast thou mad,
That thus so madly thou didst answer me?

DROMIO OF SYRACUSE
What answer, sir? when spake I such a word?

ANTIPHOLUS OF SYRACUSE
Even now, even here, not half an hour since.

DROMIO OF SYRACUSE
I did not see you since you sent me hence,
Home to the Centaur, with the gold you gave me.

ANTIPHOLUS OF SYRACUSE
Villain, thou didst deny the gold's receipt,
And told'st me of a mistress and a dinner;
For which, I hope, thou felt'st I was displeased.

DROMIO OF SYRACUSE
I am glad to see you in this merry vein:

What means this jest? I pray you, master, tell me.

ANTIPHOLUS OF SYRACUSE
Yea, dost thou jeer and flout me in the teeth?
Think'st thou I jest? Hold, take thou that, and that.

Beating him

DROMIO OF SYRACUSE
Hold, sir, for God's sake! now your jest is earnest:
Upon what bargain do you give it me?

ANTIPHOLUS OF SYRACUSE
Because that I familiarly sometimes
Do use you for my fool and chat with you,
Your sauciness will jest upon my love
And make a common of my serious hours.
When the sun shines let foolish gnats make sport,
But creep in crannies when he hides his beams.
If you will jest with me, know my aspect,
And fashion your demeanor to my looks,
Or I will beat this method in your sconce.

DROMIO OF SYRACUSE
Sconce call you it? so you would leave battering, I
had rather have it a head: an you use these blows
long, I must get a sconce for my head and ensconce
it too; or else I shall seek my wit in my shoulders.
But, I pray, sir why am I beaten?

ANTIPHOLUS OF SYRACUSE
Dost thou not know?

DROMIO OF SYRACUSE
Nothing, sir, but that I am beaten.

ANTIPHOLUS OF SYRACUSE
Shall I tell you why?

DROMIO OF SYRACUSE
Ay, sir, and wherefore; for they say every why hath
a wherefore.

ANTIPHOLUS OF SYRACUSE
Why, first,--for flouting me; and then, wherefore--
For urging it the second time to me.

DROMIO OF SYRACUSE
Was there ever any man thus beaten out of season,
When in the why and the wherefore is neither rhyme
nor reason?
Well, sir, I thank you.

ANTIPHOLUS OF SYRACUSE
Thank me, sir, for what?

DROMIO OF SYRACUSE
Marry, sir, for this something that you gave me for
nothing.

ANTIPHOLUS OF SYRACUSE
I'll make you amends next, to give you nothing for
something. But say, sir, is it dinner-time?

DROMIO OF SYRACUSE
No, sir; I think the meat wants that I have.

ANTIPHOLUS OF SYRACUSE
In good time, sir; what's that?

DROMIO OF SYRACUSE
Basting.

ANTIPHOLUS OF SYRACUSE
Well, sir, then 'twill be dry.

DROMIO OF SYRACUSE
If it be, sir, I pray you, eat none of it.

ANTIPHOLUS OF SYRACUSE
Your reason?

DROMIO OF SYRACUSE
Lest it make you choleric and purchase me another
dry basting.

ANTIPHOLUS OF SYRACUSE
Well, sir, learn to jest in good time: there's a
time for all things.

DROMIO OF SYRACUSE
I durst have denied that, before you were so choleric.

ANTIPHOLUS OF SYRACUSE
By what rule, sir?

DROMIO OF SYRACUSE
Marry, sir, by a rule as plain as the plain bald
pate of father Time himself.

ANTIPHOLUS OF SYRACUSE
Let's hear it.

DROMIO OF SYRACUSE
There's no time for a man to recover his hair that
grows bald by nature.

ANTIPHOLUS OF SYRACUSE
May he not do it by fine and recovery?

DROMIO OF SYRACUSE
Yes, to pay a fine for a periwig and recover the
lost hair of another man.

ANTIPHOLUS OF SYRACUSE
Why is Time such a niggard of hair, being, as it is,
so plentiful an excrement?

DROMIO OF SYRACUSE
Because it is a blessing that he bestows on beasts;
and what he hath scanted men in hair he hath given
them in wit.

ANTIPHOLUS OF SYRACUSE
Why, but there's many a man hath more hair than
wit.

DROMIO OF SYRACUSE
Not a man of those but he hath the wit to lose his
hair.

ANTIPHOLUS OF SYRACUSE
Why, thou didst conclude hairy men plain dealers
without wit.

DROMIO OF SYRACUSE
The plainer dealer, the sooner lost: yet he loseth it in a
kind of jollity.

ANTIPHOLUS OF SYRACUSE
For what reason?

DROMIO OF SYRACUSE
For two; and sound ones too.

ANTIPHOLUS OF SYRACUSE
Nay, not sound, I pray you.

DROMIO OF SYRACUSE
Sure ones, then.

ANTIPHOLUS OF SYRACUSE
Nay, not sure, in a thing falsing.

DROMIO OF SYRACUSE
Certain ones then.

ANTIPHOLUS OF SYRACUSE
Name them.

DROMIO OF SYRACUSE
The one, to save the money that he spends in
trimming; the other, that at dinner they should not
drop in his porridge.

ANTIPHOLUS OF SYRACUSE
You would all this time have proved there is no
time for all things.

DROMIO OF SYRACUSE
Marry, and did, sir; namely, no time to recover hair
lost by nature.

ANTIPHOLUS OF SYRACUSE
But your reason was not substantial, why there is no
time to recover.

DROMIO OF SYRACUSE
Thus I mend it: Time himself is bald and therefore
to the world's end will have bald followers.

ANTIPHOLUS OF SYRACUSE
I knew 'twould be a bald conclusion:
But, soft! who wafts us yonder?

Enter ADRIANA and LUCIANA

ADRIANA
Ay, ay, Antipholus, look strange and frown:
Some other mistress hath thy sweet aspects;
I am not Adriana nor thy wife.
The time was once when thou unurged wouldst vow
That never words were music to thine ear,
That never object pleasing in thine eye,
That never touch well welcome to thy hand,

That never meat sweet-savor'd in thy taste,
Unless I spake, or look'd, or touch'd, or carved to thee.
How comes it now, my husband, O, how comes it,
That thou art thus estranged from thyself?
Thyself I call it, being strange to me,
That, undividable, incorporate,
Am better than thy dear self's better part.
Ah, do not tear away thyself from me!
For know, my love, as easy mayest thou fall
A drop of water in the breaking gulf,
And take unmingled that same drop again,
Without addition or diminishing,
As take from me thyself and not me too.
How dearly would it touch me to the quick,
Shouldst thou but hear I were licentious
And that this body, consecrate to thee,
By ruffian lust should be contaminate!
Wouldst thou not spit at me and spurn at me
And hurl the name of husband in my face
And tear the stain'd skin off my harlot-brow
And from my false hand cut the wedding-ring
And break it with a deep-divorcing vow?
I know thou canst; and therefore see thou do it.
I am possess'd with an adulterate blot;
My blood is mingled with the crime of lust:
For if we too be one and thou play false,
I do digest the poison of thy flesh,
Being strumpeted by thy contagion.
Keep then far league and truce with thy true bed;
I live unstain'd, thou undishonoured.

ANTIPHOLUS OF SYRACUSE
Plead you to me, fair dame? I know you not:
In Ephesus I am but two hours old,
As strange unto your town as to your talk;
Who, every word by all my wit being scann'd,
Want wit in all one word to understand.

LUCIANA
Fie, brother! how the world is changed with you!
When were you wont to use my sister thus?
She sent for you by Dromio home to dinner.

ANTIPHOLUS OF SYRACUSE
By Dromio?

DROMIO OF SYRACUSE
By me?

ADRIANA
By thee; and this thou didst return from him,
That he did buffet thee, and, in his blows,
Denied my house for his, me for his wife.

ANTIPHOLUS OF SYRACUSE
Did you converse, sir, with this gentlewoman?
What is the course and drift of your compact?

DROMIO OF SYRACUSE
I, sir? I never saw her till this time.

ANTIPHOLUS OF SYRACUSE
Villain, thou liest; for even her very words
Didst thou deliver to me on the mart.

DROMIO OF SYRACUSE
I never spake with her in all my life.

ANTIPHOLUS OF SYRACUSE
How can she thus then call us by our names,
Unless it be by inspiration.

ADRIANA
How ill agrees it with your gravity
To counterfeit thus grossly with your slave,
Abetting him to thwart me in my mood!
Be it my wrong you are from me exempt,

But wrong not that wrong with a more contempt.
Come, I will fasten on this sleeve of thine:
Thou art an elm, my husband, I a vine,
Whose weakness, married to thy stronger state,
Makes me with thy strength to communicate:
If aught possess thee from me, it is dross,
Usurping ivy, brier, or idle moss;
Who, all for want of pruning, with intrusion
Infect thy sap and live on thy confusion.

ANTIPHOLUS OF SYRACUSE
To me she speaks; she moves me for her theme:
What, was I married to her in my dream?
Or sleep I now and think I hear all this?
What error drives our eyes and ears amiss?
Until I know this sure uncertainty,
I'll entertain the offer'd fallacy.

LUCIANA
Dromio, go bid the servants spread for dinner.

DROMIO OF SYRACUSE
O, for my beads! I cross me for a sinner.
This is the fairy land: O spite of spites!
We talk with goblins, owls and sprites:
If we obey them not, this will ensue,
They'll suck our breath, or pinch us black and blue.

LUCIANA
Why pratest thou to thyself and answer'st not?
Dromio, thou drone, thou snail, thou slug, thou sot!

DROMIO OF SYRACUSE
I am transformed, master, am I not?

ANTIPHOLUS OF SYRACUSE
I think thou art in mind, and so am I.

DROMIO OF SYRACUSE
Nay, master, both in mind and in my shape.

ANTIPHOLUS OF SYRACUSE
Thou hast thine own form.

DROMIO OF SYRACUSE
No, I am an ape.

LUCIANA
If thou art changed to aught, 'tis to an ass.

DROMIO OF SYRACUSE
'Tis true; she rides me and I long for grass.
'Tis so, I am an ass; else it could never be
But I should know her as well as she knows me.

ADRIANA
Come, come, no longer will I be a fool,
To put the finger in the eye and weep,
Whilst man and master laugh my woes to scorn.
Come, sir, to dinner. Dromio, keep the gate.
Husband, I'll dine above with you to-day
And shrive you of a thousand idle pranks.
Sirrah, if any ask you for your master,
Say he dines forth, and let no creature enter.
Come, sister. Dromio, play the porter well.

ANTIPHOLUS OF SYRACUSE
Am I in earth, in heaven, or in hell?
Sleeping or waking? mad or well-advised?
Known unto these, and to myself disguised!
I'll say as they say and persever so,
And in this mist at all adventures go.

DROMIO OF SYRACUSE
Master, shall I be porter at the gate?

ADRIANA
Ay; and let none enter, lest I break your pate.

LUCIANA
Come, come, Antipholus, we dine too late.

Exeunt

ACT III

SCENE I. Before the house of ANTIPHOLUS of Ephesus.

Enter ANTIPHOLUS of Ephesus, DROMIO of Ephesus, ANGELO, and BALTHAZAR

ANTIPHOLUS OF EPHESUS
Good Signior Angelo, you must excuse us all;
My wife is shrewish when I keep not hours:
Say that I linger'd with you at your shop
To see the making of her carcanet,
And that to-morrow you will bring it home.
But here's a villain that would face me down
He met me on the mart, and that I beat him,
And charged him with a thousand marks in gold,
And that I did deny my wife and house.
Thou drunkard, thou, what didst thou mean by this?

DROMIO OF EPHESUS
Say what you will, sir, but I know what I know;
That you beat me at the mart, I have your hand to show:
If the skin were parchment, and the blows you gave
were ink, Your own handwriting would tell you what I think.

ANTIPHOLUS OF EPHESUS
I think thou art an ass.

DROMIO OF EPHESUS
Marry, so it doth appear
By the wrongs I suffer and the blows I bear.
I should kick, being kick'd; and, being at that pass,
You would keep from my heels and beware of an ass.

ANTIPHOLUS OF EPHESUS
You're sad, Signior Balthazar: pray God our cheer
May answer my good will and your good welcome here.

BALTHAZAR
I hold your dainties cheap, sir, and your
welcome dear.

ANTIPHOLUS OF EPHESUS
O, Signior Balthazar, either at flesh or fish,
A table full of welcome make scarce one dainty dish.

BALTHAZAR
Good meat, sir, is common; that every churl affords.

ANTIPHOLUS OF EPHESUS
And welcome more common; for that's nothing but
words.

BALTHAZAR
Small cheer and great welcome makes a merry feast.

ANTIPHOLUS OF EPHESUS
Ay, to a niggardly host, and more sparing guest:
But though my cates be mean, take them in good part;
Better cheer may you have, but not with better heart.
But, soft! my door is lock'd. Go bid them let us in.

DROMIO OF EPHESUS
Maud, Bridget, Marian, Cicel, Gillian, Ginn!

DROMIO OF SYRACUSE
[Within] Mome, malt-horse, capon, coxcomb, idiot,
patch!
Either get thee from the door, or sit down at the
hatch.
Dost thou conjure for wenches, that thou call'st for
such store,

When one is one too many? Go, get thee from the door.

DROMIO OF EPHESUS
What patch is made our porter? My master stays in the street.

DROMIO OF SYRACUSE
[Within] Let him walk from whence he came, lest he catch cold on's feet.

ANTIPHOLUS OF EPHESUS
Who talks within there? ho, open the door!

DROMIO OF SYRACUSE
[Within] Right, sir; I'll tell you when, an you tell me wherefore.

ANTIPHOLUS OF EPHESUS
Wherefore? for my dinner: I have not dined to-day.

DROMIO OF SYRACUSE
[Within] Nor to-day here you must not; come again when you may.

ANTIPHOLUS OF EPHESUS
What art thou that keepest me out from the house I owe?

DROMIO OF SYRACUSE
[Within] The porter for this time, sir, and my name is Dromio.

DROMIO OF EPHESUS
O villain! thou hast stolen both mine office and my name.
The one ne'er got me credit, the other mickle blame.
If thou hadst been Dromio to-day in my place,
Thou wouldst have changed thy face for a name or thy

name for an ass.

LUCE
[Within] What a coil is there, Dromio? who are those
at the gate?

DROMIO OF EPHESUS
Let my master in, Luce.

LUCE
[Within] Faith, no; he comes too late;
And so tell your master.

DROMIO OF EPHESUS
O Lord, I must laugh!
Have at you with a proverb--Shall I set in my staff?

LUCE
[Within] Have at you with another; that's--When?
can you tell?

DROMIO OF SYRACUSE
[Within] If thy name be call'd Luce--Luce, thou hast
answered him well.

ANTIPHOLUS OF EPHESUS
Do you hear, you minion? you'll let us in, I hope?

LUCE
[Within] I thought to have asked you.

DROMIO OF SYRACUSE
[Within] And you said no.

DROMIO OF EPHESUS
So, come, help: well struck! there was blow for blow.

ANTIPHOLUS OF EPHESUS
Thou baggage, let me in.

LUCE
[Within] Can you tell for whose sake?

DROMIO OF EPHESUS
Master, knock the door hard.

LUCE
[Within] Let him knock till it ache.
ANTIPHOLUS

OF EPHESUS
You'll cry for this, minion, if I beat the door down.

LUCE
[Within] What needs all that, and a pair of stocks in
the town?

ADRIANA
[Within] Who is that at the door that keeps all this
noise?

DROMIO OF SYRACUSE
[Within] By my troth, your town is troubled with
unruly boys.

ANTIPHOLUS OF EPHESUS
Are you there, wife? you might have come before.

ADRIANA
[Within] Your wife, sir knave! go get you from the door.

DROMIO OF EPHESUS
If you went in pain, master, this 'knave' would go sore.

ANGELO
Here is neither cheer, sir, nor welcome: we would
fain have either.

BALTHAZAR
In debating which was best, we shall part with
neither.

DROMIO OF EPHESUS
They stand at the door, master; bid them welcome
hither.

ANTIPHOLUS OF EPHESUS
There is something in the wind, that we cannot get in.

DROMIO OF EPHESUS
You would say so, master, if your garments were thin.
Your cake there is warm within; you stand here in the
cold:
It would make a man mad as a buck, to be so bought
and sold.

ANTIPHOLUS OF EPHESUS
Go fetch me something: I'll break ope the gate.

DROMIO OF SYRACUSE
[Within] Break any breaking here, and I'll break your
knave's pate.

DROMIO OF EPHESUS
A man may break a word with you, sir, and words are
but wind,
Ay, and break it in your face, so he break it not
behind.

DROMIO OF SYRACUSE
[Within] It seems thou want'st breaking: out upon
thee, hind!

DROMIO OF EPHESUS
Here's too much 'out upon thee!' I pray thee, let me in.

DROMIO OF SYRACUSE
[Within] Ay, when fowls have no feathers and fish have
no fin.

ANTIPHOLUS OF EPHESUS
Well, I'll break in: go borrow me a crow.

DROMIO OF EPHESUS
A crow without feather? Master, mean you so?
For a fish without a fin, there's a fowl without a
feather;
If a crow help us in, sirrah, we'll pluck a crow
together.

ANTIPHOLUS OF EPHESUS
Go get thee gone; fetch me an iron crow.

BALTHAZAR
Have patience, sir; O, let it not be so!
Herein you war against your reputation
And draw within the compass of suspect
The unviolated honour of your wife.
Once this,--your long experience of her wisdom,
Her sober virtue, years and modesty,
Plead on her part some cause to you unknown:
And doubt not, sir, but she will well excuse
Why at this time the doors are made against you.
Be ruled by me: depart in patience,
And let us to the Tiger all to dinner,
And about evening come yourself alone
To know the reason of this strange restraint.
If by strong hand you offer to break in
Now in the stirring passage of the day,
A vulgar comment will be made of it,
And that supposed by the common rout
Against your yet ungalled estimation

That may with foul intrusion enter in
And dwell upon your grave when you are dead;
For slander lives upon succession,
For ever housed where it gets possession.

ANTIPHOLUS OF EPHESUS
You have prevailed: I will depart in quiet,
And, in despite of mirth, mean to be merry.
I know a wench of excellent discourse,
Pretty and witty; wild, and yet, too, gentle:
There will we dine. This woman that I mean,
My wife--but, I protest, without desert--
Hath oftentimes upbraided me withal:
To her will we to dinner.

To Angelo

Get you home
And fetch the chain; by this I know 'tis made:
Bring it, I pray you, to the Porpentine;
For there's the house: that chain will I bestow--
Be it for nothing but to spite my wife--
Upon mine hostess there: good sir, make haste.
Since mine own doors refuse to entertain me,
I'll knock elsewhere, to see if they'll disdain me.

ANGELO
I'll meet you at that place some hour hence.
ANTIPHOLUS

OF EPHESUS
Do so. This jest shall cost me some expense.

Exeunt

SCENE II. The same.

Enter LUCIANA and ANTIPHOLUS of Syracuse

LUCIANA
And may it be that you have quite forgot
A husband's office? shall, Antipholus.
Even in the spring of love, thy love-springs rot?
Shall love, in building, grow so ruinous?
If you did wed my sister for her wealth,
Then for her wealth's sake use her with more
kindness:
Or if you like elsewhere, do it by stealth;
Muffle your false love with some show of blindness:
Let not my sister read it in your eye;
Be not thy tongue thy own shame's orator;
Look sweet, be fair, become disloyalty;
Apparel vice like virtue's harbinger;
Bear a fair presence, though your heart be tainted;
Teach sin the carriage of a holy saint;
Be secret-false: what need she be acquainted?
What simple thief brags of his own attaint?
'Tis double wrong, to truant with your bed
And let her read it in thy looks at board:
Shame hath a bastard fame, well managed;
Ill d eeds are doubled with an evil word.
Alas, poor women! make us but believe,
Being compact of credit, that you love us;
Though others have the arm, show us the sleeve;
We in your motion turn and you may move us.
Then, gentle brother, get you in again;
Comfort my sister, cheer her, call her wife:
'Tis holy sport to be a little vain,
When the sweet breath of flattery conquers strife.

ANTIPHOLUS OF SYRACUSE
Sweet mistress--what your name is else, I know not,
Nor by what wonder you do hit of mine,--

Less in your knowledge and your grace you show not
Than our earth's wonder, more than earth divine.
Teach me, dear creature, how to think and speak;
Lay open to my earthy-gross conceit,
Smother'd in errors, feeble, shallow, weak,
The folded meaning of your words' deceit.
Against my soul's pure truth why labour you
To make it wander in an unknown field?
Are you a god? would you create me new?
Transform me then, and to your power I'll yield.
But if that I am I, then well I know
Your weeping sister is no wife of mine,
Nor to her bed no homage do I owe
Far more, far more to you do I decline.
O, train me not, sweet mermaid, with thy note,
To drown me in thy sister's flood of tears:
Sing, siren, for thyself and I will dote:
Spread o'er the silver waves thy golden hairs,
And as a bed I'll take them and there lie,
And in that glorious supposition think
He gains by death that hath such means to die:
Let Love, being light, be drowned if she sink!

LUCIANA
What, are you mad, that you do reason so?

ANTIPHOLUS OF SYRACUSE
Not mad, but mated; how, I do not know.

LUCIANA
It is a fault that springeth from your eye.

ANTIPHOLUS OF SYRACUSE
For gazing on your beams, fair sun, being by.

LUCIANA
Gaze where you should, and that will clear your sight.

ANTIPHOLUS OF SYRACUSE
As good to wink, sweet love, as look on night.

LUCIANA
Why call you me love? call my sister so.

ANTIPHOLUS OF SYRACUSE
Thy sister's sister.

LUCIANA
That's my sister.

ANTIPHOLUS OF SYRACUSE
No;
It is thyself, mine own self's better part,
Mine eye's clear eye, my dear heart's dearer heart,
My food, my fortune and my sweet hope's aim,
My sole earth's heaven and my heaven's claim.

LUCIANA
All this my sister is, or else should be.

ANTIPHOLUS OF SYRACUSE
Call thyself sister, sweet, for I am thee.
Thee will I love and with thee lead my life:
Thou hast no husband yet nor I no wife.
Give me thy hand.

LUCIANA
O, soft, air! hold you still:
I'll fetch my sister, to get her good will.

Exit

Enter DROMIO of Syracuse

ANTIPHOLUS OF SYRACUSE
Why, how now, Dromio! where runn'st thou so fast?

DROMIO OF SYRACUSE
Do you know me, sir? am I Dromio? am I your man?
am I myself?

ANTIPHOLUS OF SYRACUSE
Thou art Dromio, thou art my man, thou art thyself.

DROMIO OF SYRACUSE
I am an ass, I am a woman's man and besides myself.

ANTIPHOLUS OF SYRACUSE
What woman's man? and how besides thyself? besides
thyself?

DROMIO OF SYRACUSE
Marry, sir, besides myself, I am due to a woman; one
that claims me, one that haunts me, one that will
have me.

ANTIPHOLUS OF SYRACUSE
What claim lays she to thee?

DROMIO OF SYRACUSE
Marry sir, such claim as you would lay to your
horse; and she would have me as a beast: not that, I
being a beast, she would have me; but that she,
being a very beastly creature, lays claim to me.

ANTIPHOLUS OF SYRACUSE
What is she?

DROMIO OF SYRACUSE
A very reverent body; ay, such a one as a man may
not speak of without he say 'Sir-reverence.' I have
but lean luck in the match, and yet is she a
wondrous fat marriage.

ANTIPHOLUS OF SYRACUSE
How dost thou mean a fat marriage?

DROMIO OF SYRACUSE
Marry, sir, she's the kitchen wench and all grease;
and I know not what use to put her to but to make a
lamp of her and run from her by her own light. I
warrant, her rags and the tallow in them will burn a
Poland winter: if she lives till doomsday,
she'll burn a week longer than the whole world.

ANTIPHOLUS OF SYRACUSE
What complexion is she of?

DROMIO OF SYRACUSE
Swart, like my shoe, but her face nothing half so
clean kept: for why, she sweats; a man may go over
shoes in the grime of it.

ANTIPHOLUS OF SYRACUSE
That's a fault that water will mend.

DROMIO OF SYRACUSE
No, sir, 'tis in grain; Noah's flood could not do it.

ANTIPHOLUS OF SYRACUSE
What's her name?

DROMIO OF SYRACUSE
Nell, sir; but her name and three quarters, that's an
ell and three quarters, will not measure her from hip
to hip.

ANTIPHOLUS OF SYRACUSE
Then she bears some breadth?

DROMIO OF SYRACUSE
No longer from head to foot than from hip to hip:
she is spherical, like a globe; I could find out
countries in her.

ANTIPHOLUS OF SYRACUSE
In what part of her body stands Ireland?

DROMIO OF SYRACUSE
Marry, in her buttocks: I found it out by the bogs.

ANTIPHOLUS OF SYRACUSE
Where Scotland?

DROMIO OF SYRACUSE
I found it by the barrenness; hard in the palm of the
hand.

ANTIPHOLUS OF SYRACUSE
Where France?

DROMIO OF SYRACUSE
In her forehead; armed and reverted, making war
against her heir.

ANTIPHOLUS OF SYRACUSE
Where England?

DROMIO OF SYRACUSE
I looked for the chalky cliffs, but I could find no
whiteness in them; but I guess it stood in her chin,
by the salt rheum that ran between France and it.

ANTIPHOLUS OF SYRACUSE
Where Spain?

DROMIO OF SYRACUSE
Faith, I saw it not; but I felt it hot in her breath.

ANTIPHOLUS OF SYRACUSE
Where America, the Indies?

DROMIO OF SYRACUSE
Oh, sir, upon her nose all o'er embellished with

rubies, carbuncles, sapphires, declining their rich
aspect to the hot breath of Spain; who sent whole
armadoes of caracks to be ballast at her nose.

ANTIPHOLUS OF SYRACUSE
Where stood Belgia, the Netherlands?

DROMIO OF SYRACUSE
Oh, sir, I did not look so low. To conclude, this
drudge, or diviner, laid claim to me, call'd me
Dromio; swore I was assured to her; told me what
privy marks I had about me, as, the mark of my
shoulder, the mole in my neck, the great wart on my
left arm, that I amazed ran from her as a witch:
And, I think, if my breast had not been made of
faith and my heart of steel,
She had transform'd me to a curtal dog and made
me turn i' the wheel.

ANTIPHOLUS OF SYRACUSE
Go hie thee presently, post to the road:
An if the wind blow any way from shore,
I will not harbour in this town to-night:
If any bark put forth, come to the mart,
Where I will walk till thou return to me.
If every one knows us and we know none,
'Tis time, I think, to trudge, pack and be gone.

DROMIO OF SYRACUSE
As from a bear a man would run for life,
So fly I from her that would be my wife.

Exit

ANTIPHOLUS OF SYRACUSE
There's none but witches do inhabit here;
And therefore 'tis high time that I were hence.
She that doth call me husband, even my soul

Doth for a wife abhor. But her fair sister,
Possess'd with such a gentle sovereign grace,
Of such enchanting presence and discourse,
Hath almost made me traitor to myself:
But, lest myself be guilty to self-wrong,
I'll stop mine ears against the mermaid's song.

Enter ANGELO with the chain

ANGELO
Master Antipholus,--

ANTIPHOLUS OF SYRACUSE
Ay, that's my name.

ANGELO
I know it well, sir, lo, here is the chain.
I thought to have ta'en you at the Porpentine:
The chain unfinish'd made me stay thus long.

ANTIPHOLUS OF SYRACUSE
What is your will that I shall do with this?

ANGELO
What please yourself, sir: I have made it for you.

ANTIPHOLUS OF SYRACUSE
Made it for me, sir! I bespoke it not.

ANGELO
Not once, nor twice, but twenty times you have.
Go home with it and please your wife withal;
And soon at supper-time I'll visit you
And then receive my money for the chain.

ANTIPHOLUS OF SYRACUSE
I pray you, sir, receive the money now,
For fear you ne'er see chain nor money more.

ANGELO
You are a merry man, sir: fare you well.

Exit

ANTIPHOLUS OF SYRACUSE
What I should think of this, I cannot tell:
But this I think, there's no man is so vain
That would refuse so fair an offer'd chain.
I see a man here needs not live by shifts,
When in the streets he meets such golden gifts.
I'll to the mart, and there for Dromio stay
If any ship put out, then straight away.

Exit

ACT IV

SCENE I. A public place.

Enter Second Merchant, ANGELO, and an Officer

Second Merchant
You know since Pentecost the sum is due,
And since I have not much importuned you;
Nor now I had not, but that I am bound
To Persia, and want guilders for my voyage:
Therefore make present satisfaction,
Or I'll attach you by this officer.

ANGELO
Even just the sum that I do owe to you
Is growing to me by Antipholus,
And in the instant that I met with you
He had of me a chain: at five o'clock
I shall receive the money for the same.
Pleaseth you walk with me down to his house,
I will discharge my bond and thank you too.

*Enter ANTIPHOLUS of Ephesus and DROMIO of
Ephesus from the courtezan's*

Officer
That labour may you save: see where he comes.

ANTIPHOLUS OF EPHESUS
While I go to the goldsmith's house, go thou
And buy a rope's end: that will I bestow
Among my wife and her confederates,
For locking me out of my doors by day.
But, soft! I see the goldsmith. Get thee gone;
Buy thou a rope and bring it home to me.

DROMIO OF EPHESUS
I buy a thousand pound a year: I buy a rope.

Exit

ANTIPHOLUS OF EPHESUS
A man is well holp up that trusts to you:
I promised your presence and the chain;
But neither chain nor goldsmith came to me.
Belike you thought our love would last too long,
If it were chain'd together, and therefore came not.

ANGELO
Saving your merry humour, here's the note
How much your chain weighs to the utmost carat,
The fineness of the gold and chargeful fashion.
Which doth amount to three odd ducats more
Than I stand debted to this gentleman:
I pray you, see him presently discharged,
For he is bound to sea and stays but for it.

ANTIPHOLUS OF EPHESUS
I am not furnish'd with the present money;
Besides, I have some business in the town.
Good signior, take the stranger to my house
And with you take the chain and bid my wife
Disburse the sum on the receipt thereof:
Perchance I will be there as soon as you.

ANGELO
Then you will bring the chain to her yourself?

ANTIPHOLUS OF EPHESUS
No; bear it with you, lest I come not time enough.

ANGELO
Well, sir, I will. Have you the chain about you?

ANTIPHOLUS OF EPHESUS
An if I have not, sir, I hope you have;
Or else you may return without your money.

ANGELO
Nay, come, I pray you, sir, give me the chain:
Both wind and tide stays for this gentleman,
And I, to blame, have held him here too long.

ANTIPHOLUS OF EPHESUS
Good Lord! you use this dalliance to excuse
Your breach of promise to the Porpentine.
I should have chid you for not bringing it,
But, like a shrew, you first begin to brawl.

Second Merchant
The hour steals on; I pray you, sir, dispatch.

ANGELO
You hear how he importunes me;--the chain!

ANTIPHOLUS OF EPHESUS
Why, give it to my wife and fetch your money.

ANGELO
Come, come, you know I gave it you even now.
Either send the chain or send me by some token.

ANTIPHOLUS OF EPHESUS
Fie, now you run this humour out of breath,
where's the chain? I pray you, let me see it.

Second Merchant
My business cannot brook this dalliance.
Good sir, say whether you'll answer me or no:
If not, I'll leave him to the officer.

ANTIPHOLUS OF EPHESUS
I answer you! what should I answer you?

ANGELO
The money that you owe me for the chain.

ANTIPHOLUS OF EPHESUS
I owe you none till I receive the chain.

ANGELO
You know I gave it you half an hour since.

ANTIPHOLUS OF EPHESUS
You gave me none: you wrong me much to say so.

ANGELO
You wrong me more, sir, in denying it:
Consider how it stands upon my credit.

Second Merchant
Well, officer, arrest him at my suit.

Officer
I do; and charge you in the duke's name to obey me.

ANGELO
This touches me in reputation.
Either consent to pay this sum for me
Or I attach you by this officer.

ANTIPHOLUS OF EPHESUS
Consent to pay thee that I never had!
Arrest me, foolish fellow, if thou darest.

ANGELO
Here is thy fee; arrest him, officer,
I would not spare my brother in this case,
If he should scorn me so apparently.

Officer
I do arrest you, sir: you hear the suit.

ANTIPHOLUS OF EPHESUS
I do obey thee till I give thee bail.
But, sirrah, you shall buy this sport as dear
As all the metal in your shop will answer.

ANGELO
Sir, sir, I will have law in Ephesus,
To your notorious shame; I doubt it not.

Enter DROMIO of Syracuse, from the bay

DROMIO OF SYRACUSE
Master, there is a bark of Epidamnum
That stays but till her owner comes aboard,
And then, sir, she bears away. Our fraughtage, sir,
I have convey'd aboard; and I have bought
The oil, the balsamum and aqua-vitae.
The ship is in her trim; the merry wind
Blows fair from land: they stay for nought at all
But for their owner, master, and yourself.

ANTIPHOLUS OF EPHESUS
How now! a madman! Why, thou peevish sheep,
What ship of Epidamnum stays for me?

DROMIO OF SYRACUSE
A ship you sent me to, to hire waftage.

ANTIPHOLUS OF EPHESUS
Thou drunken slave, I sent thee for a rope;
And told thee to what purpose and what end.

DROMIO OF SYRACUSE
You sent me for a rope's end as soon:
You sent me to the bay, sir, for a bark.

ANTIPHOLUS OF EPHESUS
I will debate this matter at more leisure
And teach your ears to list me with more heed.
To Adriana, villain, hie thee straight:
Give her this key, and tell her, in the desk
That's cover'd o'er with Turkish tapestry,
There is a purse of ducats; let her send it:
Tell her I am arrested in the street
And that shall bail me; hie thee, slave, be gone!
On, officer, to prison till it come.

Exeunt Second Merchant, Angelo, Officer, and
Antipholus of Ephesus

DROMIO OF SYRACUSE
To Adriana! that is where we dined,
Where Dowsabel did claim me for her husband:
She is too big, I hope, for me to compass.
Thither I must, although against my will,
For servants must their masters' minds fulfil.

Exit

SCENE II. The house of ANTIPHOLUS of Ephesus.

Enter ADRIANA and LUCIANA

ADRIANA
Ah, Luciana, did he tempt thee so?
Mightst thou perceive austerely in his eye
That he did plead in earnest? yea or no?
Look'd he or red or pale, or sad or merrily?
What observation madest thou in this case
Of his heart's meteors tilting in his face?

LUCIANA
First he denied you had in him no right.

ADRIANA
He meant he did me none; the more my spite.

LUCIANA
Then swore he that he was a stranger here.

ADRIANA
And true he swore, though yet forsworn he were.

LUCIANA
Then pleaded I for you.

ADRIANA
And what said he?

LUCIANA
That love I begg'd for you he begg'd of me.

ADRIANA
With what persuasion did he tempt thy love?

LUCIANA
With words that in an honest suit might move.

First he did praise my beauty, then my speech.

ADRIANA
Didst speak him fair?

LUCIANA
Have patience, I beseech.

ADRIANA
I cannot, nor I will not, hold me still;
My tongue, though not my heart, shall have his will.
He is deformed, crooked, old and sere,
Ill-faced, worse bodied, shapeless everywhere;
Vicious, ungentle, foolish, blunt, unkind;
Stigmatical in making, worse in mind.

LUCIANA
Who would be jealous then of such a one?
No evil lost is wail'd when it is gone.

ADRIANA
Ah, but I think him better than I say,
And yet would herein others' eyes were worse.
Far from her nest the lapwing cries away:
My heart prays for him, though my tongue do curse.

Enter DROMIO of Syracuse

DROMIO OF SYRACUSE
Here! go; the desk, the purse! sweet, now, make haste.

LUCIANA
How hast thou lost thy breath?

DROMIO OF SYRACUSE
By running fast.

ADRIANA
Where is thy master, Dromio? is he well?

DROMIO OF SYRACUSE
No, he's in Tartar limbo, worse than hell.
A devil in an everlasting garment hath him;
One whose hard heart is button'd up with steel;
A fiend, a fury, pitiless and rough;
A wolf, nay, worse, a fellow all in buff;
A back-friend, a shoulder-clapper, one that
countermands
The passages of alleys, creeks and narrow lands;
A hound that runs counter and yet draws dryfoot well;
One that before the judgement carries poor souls to
hell.

ADRIANA
Why, man, what is the matter?

DROMIO OF SYRACUSE
I do not know the matter: he is 'rested on the case.

ADRIANA
What, is he arrested? Tell me at whose suit.

DROMIO OF SYRACUSE
I know not at whose suit he is arrested well;
But he's in a suit of buff which 'rested him, that can I
tell.
Will you send him, mistress, redemption, the money in
his desk?

ADRIANA
Go fetch it, sister.

Exit Luciana

This I wonder at,
That he, unknown to me, should be in debt.
Tell me, was he arrested on a band?

DROMIO OF SYRACUSE
Not on a band, but on a stronger thing;
A chain, a chain! Do you not hear it ring?

ADRIANA
What, the chain?

DROMIO OF SYRACUSE
No, no, the bell: 'tis time that I were gone:
It was two ere I left him, and now the clock
strikes one.

ADRIANA
The hours come back! that did I never hear.

DROMIO OF SYRACUSE
O, yes; if any hour meet a sergeant, a' turns back for
very fear.

ADRIANA
As if Time were in debt! how fondly dost thou reason!

DROMIO OF SYRACUSE
Time is a very bankrupt, and owes more than he's
worth, to season.
Nay, he's a thief too: have you not heard men say
That Time comes stealing on by night and day?
If Time be in debt and theft, and a sergeant in the
way,
Hath he not reason to turn back an hour in a day?

Re-enter LUCIANA with a purse

ADRIANA
Go, Dromio; there's the money, bear it straight;
And bring thy master home immediately.
Come, sister: I am press'd down with conceit--
Conceit, my comfort and my injury.
Exeunt

SCENE III. A public place.

Enter ANTIPHOLUS of Syracuse

ANTIPHOLUS OF SYRACUSE
There's not a man I meet but doth salute me
As if I were their well-acquainted friend;
And every one doth call me by my name.
Some tender money to me; some invite me;
Some other give me thanks for kindnesses;
Some offer me commodities to buy:
Even now a tailor call'd me in his shop
And show'd me silks that he had bought for me,
And therewithal took measure of my body.
Sure, these are but imaginary wiles
And Lapland sorcerers inhabit here.

Enter DROMIO OF SYRACUSE

DROMIO OF SYRACUSE
Master, here's the gold you sent me for. What, have
you got the picture of old Adam new-apparelled?

ANTIPHOLUS OF SYRACUSE
What gold is this? what Adam dost thou mean?

DROMIO OF SYRACUSE
Not that Adam that kept the Paradise but that Adam
that keeps the prison: he that goes in the calf's
skin that was killed for the Prodigal; he that came
behind you, sir, like an evil angel, and bid you
forsake your liberty.

ANTIPHOLUS OF SYRACUSE
I understand thee not.

DROMIO OF SYRACUSE
No? why, 'tis a plain case: he that went, like a
bass-viol, in a case of leather; the man, sir,
that, when gentlemen are tired, gives them a sob
and 'rests them; he, sir, that takes pity on decayed
men and gives them suits of durance; he that sets up
his rest to do more exploits with his mace than a
morris-pike.

ANTIPHOLUS OF SYRACUSE

What, thou meanest an officer?

DROMIO OF SYRACUSE
Ay, sir, the sergeant of the band, he that brings
any man to answer it that breaks his band; one that
thinks a man always going to bed, and says, 'God
give you good rest!'

ANTIPHOLUS OF SYRACUSE
Well, sir, there rest in your foolery. Is there any

DROMIO OF SYRACUSE
Why, sir, I brought you word an hour since that the
bark Expedition put forth to-night; and then were
you hindered by the sergeant, to tarry for the hoy
Delay. Here are the angels that you sent for to
deliver you.

ANTIPHOLUS OF SYRACUSE
The fellow is distract, and so am I;
And here we wander in illusions:
Some blessed power deliver us from hence!

Enter a Courtezan

Courtezan
Well met, well met, Master Antipholus.
I see, sir, you have found the goldsmith now:

Is that the chain you promised me to-day?

ANTIPHOLUS OF SYRACUSE
Satan, avoid! I charge thee, tempt me not.

DROMIO OF SYRACUSE
Master, is this Mistress Satan?

ANTIPHOLUS OF SYRACUSE
It is the devil.

DROMIO OF SYRACUSE
Nay, she is worse, she is the devil's dam; and here
she comes in the habit of a light wench: and thereof
comes that the wenches say 'God damn me;' that's as
much to say 'God make me a light wench.' It is
written, they appear to men like angels of light:
light is an effect of fire, and fire will burn;
ergo, light wenches will burn. Come not near her.

Courtezan
Your man and you are marvellous merry, sir.
Will you go with me? We'll mend our dinner here?

DROMIO OF SYRACUSE
Master, if you do, expect spoon-meat; or bespeak a
long spoon.

ANTIPHOLUS OF SYRACUSE
Why, Dromio?

DROMIO OF SYRACUSE
Marry, he must have a long spoon that must eat with
the devil.

ANTIPHOLUS OF SYRACUSE
Avoid then, fiend! what tell'st thou me of supping?
Thou art, as you are all, a sorceress:
I conjure thee to leave me and be gone.

Courtezan
Give me the ring of mine you had at dinner,
Or, for my diamond, the chain you promised,
And I'll be gone, sir, and not trouble you.

DROMIO OF SYRACUSE
Some devils ask but the parings of one's nail,
A rush, a hair, a drop of blood, a pin,
A nut, a cherry-stone;
But she, more covetous, would have a chain.
Master, be wise: an if you give it her,
The devil will shake her chain and fright us with it.

Courtezan
I pray you, sir, my ring, or else the chain:
I hope you do not mean to cheat me so.

ANTIPHOLUS OF SYRACUSE
Avaunt, thou witch! Come, Dromio, let us go.

DROMIO OF SYRACUSE
'Fly pride,' says the peacock: mistress, that you know.

Exeunt Antipholus of Syracuse and Dromio of
Syracuse

Courtezan
Now, out of doubt Antipholus is mad,
Else would he never so demean himself.
A ring he hath of mine worth forty ducats,
And for the same he promised me a chain:
Both one and other he denies me now.
The reason that I gather he is mad,
Besides this present instance of his rage,
Is a mad tale he told to-day at dinner,
Of his own doors being shut against his entrance.
Belike his wife, acquainted with his fits,
On purpose shut the doors against his way.

My way is now to hie home to his house,
And tell his wife that, being lunatic,
He rush'd into my house and took perforce
My ring away. This course I fittest choose;
For forty ducats is too much to lose.

Exit

SCENE IV. A street.

Enter ANTIPHOLUS of Ephesus and the Officer

ANTIPHOLUS OF EPHESUS
Fear me not, man; I will not break away:
I'll give thee, ere I leave thee, so much money,
To warrant thee, as I am 'rested for.
My wife is in a wayward mood to-day,
And will not lightly trust the messenger
That I should be attach'd in Ephesus,
I tell you, 'twill sound harshly in her ears.

Enter DROMIO of Ephesus with a rope's-end

Here comes my man; I think he brings the money.
How now, sir! have you that I sent you for?

DROMIO OF EPHESUS
Here's that, I warrant you, will pay them all.

ANTIPHOLUS OF EPHESUS
But where's the money?

DROMIO OF EPHESUS
Why, sir, I gave the money for the rope.

ANTIPHOLUS OF EPHESUS
Five hundred ducats, villain, for a rope?

DROMIO OF EPHESUS
I'll serve you, sir, five hundred at the rate.

ANTIPHOLUS OF EPHESUS
To what end did I bid thee hie thee home?

DROMIO OF EPHESUS
To a rope's-end, sir; and to that end am I returned.

ANTIPHOLUS OF EPHESUS
And to that end, sir, I will welcome you.

Beating him

Officer
Good sir, be patient.

DROMIO OF EPHESUS
Nay, 'tis for me to be patient; I am in adversity.

Officer
Good, now, hold thy tongue.

DROMIO OF EPHESUS
Nay, rather persuade him to hold his hands.

ANTIPHOLUS OF EPHESUS
Thou whoreson, senseless villain!

DROMIO OF EPHESUS
I would I were senseless, sir, that I might not feel
your blows.

ANTIPHOLUS OF EPHESUS
Thou art sensible in nothing but blows, and so is an
ass.

DROMIO OF EPHESUS
I am an ass, indeed; you may prove it by my long
ears. I have served him from the hour of my
nativity to this instant, and have nothing at his
hands for my service but blows. When I am cold, he
heats me with beating; when I am warm, he cools me
with beating; I am waked with it when I sleep;
raised with it when I sit; driven out of doors with

it when I go from home; welcomed home with it when
I return; nay, I bear it on my shoulders, as a
beggar wont her brat; and, I think when he hath
lamed me, I shall beg with it from door to door.

ANTIPHOLUS OF EPHESUS
Come, go along; my wife is coming yonder.

Enter ADRIANA, LUCIANA, the Courtezan, and PINCH

DROMIO OF EPHESUS
Mistress, 'respice finem,' respect your end; or
rather, the prophecy like the parrot, 'beware the
rope's-end.'

ANTIPHOLUS OF EPHESUS
Wilt thou still talk?

Beating him

Courtezan
How say you now? is not your husband mad?

ADRIANA
His incivility confirms no less.
Good Doctor Pinch, you are a conjurer;
Establish him in his true sense again,
And I will please you what you will demand.

LUCIANA
Alas, how fiery and how sharp he looks!

Courtezan
Mark how he trembles in his ecstasy!

PINCH
Give me your hand and let me feel your pulse.

ANTIPHOLUS OF EPHESUS
There is my hand, and let it feel your ear.

Striking him

PINCH
I charge thee, Satan, housed within this man,
To yield possession to my holy prayers
And to thy state of darkness hie thee straight:
I conjure thee by all the saints in heaven!

ANTIPHOLUS OF EPHESUS
Peace, doting wizard, peace! I am not mad.

ADRIANA
O, that thou wert not, poor distressed soul!

ANTIPHOLUS OF EPHESUS
You minion, you, are these your customers?
Did this companion with the saffron face
Revel and feast it at my house to-day,
Whilst upon me the guilty doors were shut
And I denied to enter in my house?

ADRIANA
O husband, God doth know you dined at home;
Where would you had remain'd until this time,
Free from these slanders and this open shame!

ANTIPHOLUS OF EPHESUS
Dined at home! Thou villain, what sayest thou?

DROMIO OF EPHESUS
Sir, sooth to say, you did not dine at home.

ANTIPHOLUS OF EPHESUS
Were not my doors lock'd up and I shut out?

DROMIO OF EPHESUS
Perdie, your doors were lock'd and you shut out.

ANTIPHOLUS OF EPHESUS
And did not she herself revile me there?

DROMIO OF EPHESUS
Sans fable, she herself reviled you there.

ANTIPHOLUS OF EPHESUS
Did not her kitchen-maid rail, taunt, and scorn me?

DROMIO OF EPHESUS
Certes, she did; the kitchen-vestal scorn'd you.

ANTIPHOLUS OF EPHESUS
And did not I in rage depart from thence?

DROMIO OF EPHESUS
In verity you did; my bones bear witness,
That since have felt the vigour of his rage.

ADRIANA
Is't good to soothe him in these contraries?

PINCH
It is no shame: the fellow finds his vein,
And yielding to him humours well his frenzy.

ANTIPHOLUS OF EPHESUS
Thou hast suborn'd the goldsmith to arrest me.

ADRIANA
Alas, I sent you money to redeem you,
By Dromio here, who came in haste for it.

DROMIO OF EPHESUS
Money by me! heart and goodwill you might;
But surely master, not a rag of money.

ANTIPHOLUS OF EPHESUS
Went'st not thou to her for a purse of ducats?

ADRIANA
He came to me and I deliver'd it.

LUCIANA
And I am witness with her that she did.

DROMIO OF EPHESUS
God and the rope-maker bear me witness
That I was sent for nothing but a rope!

PINCH
Mistress, both man and master is possess'd;
I know it by their pale and deadly looks:
They must be bound and laid in some dark room.

ANTIPHOLUS OF EPHESUS
Say, wherefore didst thou lock me forth to-day?
And why dost thou deny the bag of gold?

ADRIANA
I did not, gentle husband, lock thee forth.

DROMIO OF EPHESUS
And, gentle master, I received no gold;
But I confess, sir, that we were lock'd out.

ADRIANA
Dissembling villain, thou speak'st false in both.

ANTIPHOLUS OF EPHESUS
Dissembling harlot, thou art false in all;
And art confederate with a damned pack
To make a loathsome abject scorn of me:
But with these nails I'll pluck out these false eyes
That would behold in me this shameful sport.

Enter three or four, and offer to bind him. He strives

ADRIANA
O, bind him, bind him! let him not come near me.

PINCH
More company! The fiend is strong within him.

LUCIANA
Ay me, poor man, how pale and wan he looks!

ANTIPHOLUS OF EPHESUS
What, will you murder me? Thou gaoler, thou,
I am thy prisoner: wilt thou suffer them
To make a rescue?

Officer
Masters, let him go
He is my prisoner, and you shall not have him.

PINCH
Go bind this man, for he is frantic too.

They offer to bind Dromio of Ephesus

ADRIANA
What wilt thou do, thou peevish officer?
Hast thou delight to see a wretched man
Do outrage and displeasure to himself?

Officer
He is my prisoner: if I let him go,
The debt he owes will be required of me.

ADRIANA
I will discharge thee ere I go from thee:
Bear me forthwith unto his creditor,

And, knowing how the debt grows, I will pay it.
Good master doctor, see him safe convey'd
Home to my house. O most unhappy day!

ANTIPHOLUS OF EPHESUS
O most unhappy strumpet!

DROMIO OF EPHESUS
Master, I am here entered in bond for you.

ANTIPHOLUS OF EPHESUS
Out on thee, villain! wherefore dost thou mad me?

DROMIO OF EPHESUS
Will you be bound for nothing? be mad, good master:
cry 'The devil!'

LUCIANA
God help, poor souls, how idly do they talk!

ADRIANA
Go bear him hence. Sister, go you with me.

Exeunt all but Adriana, Luciana, Officer and
Courtezan

Say now, whose suit is he arrested at?

Officer
One Angelo, a goldsmith: do you know him?

ADRIANA
I know the man. What is the sum he owes?

Officer
Two hundred ducats.

ADRIANA
Say, how grows it due?

Officer
Due for a chain your husband had of him.

ADRIANA
He did bespeak a chain for me, but had it not.

Courtezan
When as your husband all in rage to-day
Came to my house and took away my ring--
The ring I saw upon his finger now--
Straight after did I meet him with a chain.

ADRIANA
It may be so, but I did never see it.
Come, gaoler, bring me where the goldsmith is:
I long to know the truth hereof at large.

Enter ANTIPHOLUS of Syracuse with his rapier
drawn, and DROMIO of Syracuse

LUCIANA
God, for thy mercy! they are loose again.

ADRIANA
And come with naked swords.
Let's call more help to have them bound again.

Officer
Away! they'll kill us.

Exeunt all but Antipholus of Syracuse and Dromio of
Syracuse

ANTIPHOLUS OF SYRACUSE
I see these witches are afraid of swords.

DROMIO OF SYRACUSE
She that would be your wife now ran from you.

ANTIPHOLUS OF SYRACUSE
Come to the Centaur; fetch our stuff from thence:
I long that we were safe and sound aboard.

DROMIO OF SYRACUSE
Faith, stay here this night; they will surely do us
no harm: you saw they speak us fair, give us gold:
methinks they are such a gentle nation that, but for
the mountain of mad flesh that claims marriage of
me, I could find in my heart to stay here still and
turn witch.

ANTIPHOLUS OF SYRACUSE
I will not stay to-night for all the town;
Therefore away, to get our stuff aboard.

Exeunt

ACT V

SCENE I. A street before a Priory.

Enter Second Merchant and ANGELO

ANGELO
I am sorry, sir, that I have hinder'd you;
But, I protest, he had the chain of me,
Though most dishonestly he doth deny it.

Second Merchant
How is the man esteemed here in the city?

ANGELO
Of very reverend reputation, sir,
Of credit infinite, highly beloved,
Second to none that lives here in the city:
His word might bear my wealth at any time.

Second Merchant
Speak softly; yonder, as I think, he walks.

Enter ANTIPHOLUS of Syracuse and DROMIO of Syracuse

ANGELO
'Tis so; and that self chain about his neck
Which he forswore most monstrously to have.
Good sir, draw near to me, I'll speak to him.
Signior Antipholus, I wonder much
That you would put me to this shame and trouble;
And, not without some scandal to yourself,
With circumstance and oaths so to deny
This chain which now you wear so openly:
Beside the charge, the shame, imprisonment,
You have done wrong to this my honest friend,

Who, but for staying on our controversy,
Had hoisted sail and put to sea to-day:
This chain you had of me; can you deny it?

ANTIPHOLUS OF SYRACUSE
I think I had; I never did deny it.

Second Merchant
Yes, that you did, sir, and forswore it too.

ANTIPHOLUS OF SYRACUSE
Who heard me to deny it or forswear it?

Second Merchant
These ears of mine, thou know'st did hear thee.
Fie on thee, wretch! 'tis pity that thou livest
To walk where any honest man resort.

ANTIPHOLUS OF SYRACUSE
Thou art a villain to impeach me thus:
I'll prove mine honour and mine honesty
Against thee presently, if thou darest stand.

Second Merchant
I dare, and do defy thee for a villain.

They draw

Enter ADRIANA, LUCIANA, the Courtezan, and others

ADRIANA
Hold, hurt him not, for God's sake! he is mad.
Some get within him, take his sword away:
Bind Dromio too, and bear them to my house.

DROMIO OF SYRACUSE
Run, master, run; for God's sake, take a house!
This is some priory. In, or we are spoil'd!

Exeunt Antipholus of Syracuse and Dromio of
Syracuse to the Priory

Enter the Lady Abbess, AEMILIA

AEMELIA
Be quiet, people. Wherefore throng you hither?

ADRIANA
To fetch my poor distracted husband hence.
Let us come in, that we may bind him fast
And bear him home for his recovery.

ANGELO
I knew he was not in his perfect wits.

Second Merchant
I am sorry now that I did draw on him.

AEMELIA
How long hath this possession held the man?

ADRIANA
This week he hath been heavy, sour, sad,
And much different from the man he was;
But till this afternoon his passion
Ne'er brake into extremity of rage.

AEMELIA
Hath he not lost much wealth by wreck of sea?
Buried some dear friend? Hath not else his eye
Stray'd his affection in unlawful love?
A sin prevailing much in youthful men,
Who give their eyes the liberty of gazing.
Which of these sorrows is he subject to?

ADRIANA
To none of these, except it be the last;
Namely, some love that drew him oft from home.

AEMELIA
You should for that have reprehended him.

ADRIANA
Why, so I did.

AEMELIA
Ay, but not rough enough.

ADRIANA
As roughly as my modesty would let me.

AEMELIA
Haply, in private.

ADRIANA
And in assemblies too.

AEMELIA
Ay, but not enough.

ADRIANA
It was the copy of our conference:
In bed he slept not for my urging it;
At board he fed not for my urging it;
Alone, it was the subject of my theme;
In company I often glanced it;
Still did I tell him it was vile and bad.

AEMELIA
And thereof came it that the man was mad.
The venom clamours of a jealous woman
Poisons more deadly than a mad dog's tooth.
It seems his sleeps were hinder'd by thy railing,
And therefore comes it that his head is light.
Thou say'st his meat was sauced with thy
upbraidings:
Unquiet meals make ill digestions;

Thereof the raging fire of fever bred;
And what's a fever but a fit of madness?
Thou say'st his sports were hinderd by thy brawls:
Sweet recreation barr'd, what doth ensue
But moody and dull melancholy,
Kinsman to grim and comfortless despair,
And at her heels a huge infectious troop
Of pale distemperatures and foes to life?
In food, in sport and life-preserving rest
To be disturb'd, would mad or man or beast:
The consequence is then thy jealous fits
Have scared thy husband from the use of wits.

LUCIANA
She never reprehended him but mildly,
When he demean'd himself rough, rude and wildly.
Why bear you these rebukes and answer not?

ADRIANA
She did betray me to my own reproof.
Good people enter and lay hold on him.

AEMELIA
No, not a creature enters in my house.

ADRIANA
Then let your servants bring my husband forth.

AEMELIA
Neither: he took this place for sanctuary,
And it shall privilege him from your hands
Till I have brought him to his wits again,
Or lose my labour in assaying it.

ADRIANA
I will attend my husband, be his nurse,
Diet his sickness, for it is my office,
And will have no attorney but myself;
And therefore let me have him home with me.

AEMELIA
Be patient; for I will not let him stir
Till I have used the approved means I have,
With wholesome syrups, drugs and holy prayers,
To make of him a formal man again:
It is a branch and parcel of mine oath,
A charitable duty of my order.
Therefore depart and leave him here with me.

ADRIANA
I will not hence and leave my husband here:
And ill it doth beseem your holiness
To separate the husband and the wife.

AEMELIA
Be quiet and depart: thou shalt not have him.

Exit

LUCIANA
Complain unto the duke of this indignity.

ADRIANA
Come, go: I will fall prostrate at his feet
And never rise until my tears and prayers
Have won his grace to come in person hither
And take perforce my husband from the abbess.

Second Merchant
By this, I think, the dial points at five:
Anon, I'm sure, the duke himself in person
Comes this way to the melancholy vale,
The place of death and sorry execution,
Behind the ditches of the abbey here.

ANGELO
Upon what cause?

Second Merchant
To see a reverend Syracusian merchant,
Who put unluckily into this bay
Against the laws and statutes of this town,
Beheaded publicly for his offence.

ANGELO
See where they come: we will behold his death.

LUCIANA
Kneel to the duke before he pass the abbey.

Enter DUKE SOLINUS, attended; AEGEON
bareheaded; with the Headsman and other Officers

DUKE SOLINUS
Yet once again proclaim it publicly,
If any friend will pay the sum for him,
He shall not die; so much we tender him.

ADRIANA
Justice, most sacred duke, against the abbess!

DUKE SOLINUS
She is a virtuous and a reverend lady:
It cannot be that she hath done thee wrong.

ADRIANA
May it please your grace, Antipholus, my husband,
Whom I made lord of me and all I had,
At your important letters,--this ill day
A most outrageous fit of madness took him;
That desperately he hurried through the street,
With him his bondman, all as mad as he--
Doing displeasure to the citizens
By rushing in their houses, bearing thence
Rings, jewels, any thing his rage did like.
Once did I get him bound and sent him home,
Whilst to take order for the wrongs I went,

That here and there his fury had committed.
Anon, I wot not by what strong escape,
He broke from those that had the guard of him;
And with his mad attendant and himself,
Each one with ireful passion, with drawn swords,
Met us again and madly bent on us,
Chased us away; till, raising of more aid,
We came again to bind them. Then they fled
Into this abbey, whither we pursued them:
And here the abbess shuts the gates on us
And will not suffer us to fetch him out,
Nor send him forth that we may bear him hence.
Therefore, most gracious duke, with thy command
Let him be brought forth and borne hence for help.

DUKE SOLINUS
Long since thy husband served me in my wars,
And I to thee engaged a prince's word,
When thou didst make him master of thy bed,
To do him all the grace and good I could.
Go, some of you, knock at the abbey-gate
And bid the lady abbess come to me.
I will determine this before I stir.

Enter a Servant

Servant
O mistress, mistress, shift and save yourself!
My master and his man are both broke loose,
Beaten the maids a-row and bound the doctor
Whose beard they have singed off with brands of fire;
And ever, as it blazed, they threw on him
Great pails of puddled mire to quench the hair:
My master preaches patience to him and the while
His man with scissors nicks him like a fool,
And sure, unless you send some present help,
Between them they will kill the conjurer.

ADRIANA
Peace, fool! thy master and his man are here,
And that is false thou dost report to us.

Servant
Mistress, upon my life, I tell you true;
I have not breathed almost since I did see it.
He cries for you, and vows, if he can take you,
To scorch your face and to disfigure you.

Cry within

Hark, hark! I hear him, mistress. fly, be gone!

DUKE SOLINUS
Come, stand by me; fear nothing. Guard with
halberds!

ADRIANA
Ay me, it is my husband! Witness you,
That he is borne about invisible:
Even now we housed him in the abbey here;
And now he's there, past thought of human reason.

Enter ANTIPHOLUS of Ephesus and DROMIO of
Ephesus

ANTIPHOLUS OF EPHESUS
Justice, most gracious duke, O, grant me justice!
Even for the service that long since I did thee,
When I bestrid thee in the wars and took
Deep scars to save thy life; even for the blood
That then I lost for thee, now grant me justice.

AEGEON
Unless the fear of death doth make me dote,
I see my son Antipholus and Dromio.

ANTIPHOLUS OF EPHESUS
Justice, sweet prince, against that woman there!
She whom thou gavest to me to be my wife,
That hath abused and dishonour'd me
Even in the strength and height of injury!
Beyond imagination is the wrong
That she this day hath shameless thrown on me.

DUKE SOLINUS
Discover how, and thou shalt find me just.

ANTIPHOLUS OF EPHESUS
This day, great duke, she shut the doors upon me,
While she with harlots feasted in my house.

DUKE SOLINUS
A grievous fault! Say, woman, didst thou so?

ADRIANA
No, my good lord: myself, he and my sister
To-day did dine together. So befall my soul
As this is false he burdens me withal!

LUCIANA
Ne'er may I look on day, nor sleep on night,
But she tells to your highness simple truth!

ANGELO
O perjured woman! They are both forsworn:
In this the madman justly chargeth them.

ANTIPHOLUS OF EPHESUS
My liege, I am advised what I say,
Neither disturbed with the effect of wine,
Nor heady-rash, provoked with raging ire,
Albeit my wrongs might make one wiser mad.
This woman lock'd me out this day from dinner:
That goldsmith there, were he not pack'd with her,
Could witness it, for he was with me then;

Who parted with me to go fetch a chain,
Promising to bring it to the Porpentine,
Where Balthazar and I did dine together.
Our dinner done, and he not coming thither,
I went to seek him: in the street I met him
And in his company that gentleman.
There did this perjured goldsmith swear me down
That I this day of him received the chain,
Which, God he knows, I saw not: for the which
He did arrest me with an officer.
I did obey, and sent my peasant home
For certain ducats: he with none return'd
Then fairly I bespoke the officer
To go in person with me to my house.
By the way we met
My wife, her sister, and a rabble more
Of vile confederates. Along with them
They brought one Pinch, a hungry lean-faced villain,
A mere anatomy, a mountebank,
A threadbare juggler and a fortune-teller,
A needy, hollow-eyed, sharp-looking wretch,
A dead-looking man: this pernicious slave,
Forsooth, took on him as a conjurer,
And, gazing in mine eyes, feeling my pulse,
And with no face, as 'twere, outfacing me,
Cries out, I was possess'd. Then all together
They fell upon me, bound me, bore me thence
And in a dark and dankish vault at home
There left me and my man, both bound together;
Till, gnawing with my teeth my bonds in sunder,
I gain'd my freedom, and immediately
Ran hither to your grace; whom I beseech
To give me ample satisfaction
For these deep shames and great indignities.

ANGELO
My lord, in truth, thus far I witness with him,
That he dined not at home, but was lock'd out.

DUKE SOLINUS
But had he such a chain of thee or no?

ANGELO
He had, my lord: and when he ran in here,
These people saw the chain about his neck.

Second Merchant
Besides, I will be sworn these ears of mine
Heard you confess you had the chain of him
After you first forswore it on the mart:
And thereupon I drew my sword on you;
And then you fled into this abbey here,
From whence, I think, you are come by miracle.

ANTIPHOLUS OF EPHESUS
I never came within these abbey-walls,
Nor ever didst thou draw thy sword on me:
I never saw the chain, so help me Heaven!
And this is false you burden me withal.

DUKE SOLINUS
Why, what an intricate impeach is this!
I think you all have drunk of Circe's cup.
If here you housed him, here he would have been;
If he were mad, he would not plead so coldly:
You say he dined at home; the goldsmith here
Denies that saying. Sirrah, what say you?

DROMIO OF EPHESUS
Sir, he dined with her there, at the Porpentine.

Courtezan
He did, and from my finger snatch'd that ring.

ANTIPHOLUS OF EPHESUS
'Tis true, my liege; this ring I had of her.

DUKE SOLINUS
Saw'st thou him enter at the abbey here?

Courtezan
As sure, my liege, as I do see your grace.

DUKE SOLINUS
Why, this is strange. Go call the abbess hither.
I think you are all mated or stark mad.

Exit one to Abbess

AEGEON
Most mighty duke, vouchsafe me speak a word:
Haply I see a friend will save my life
And pay the sum that may deliver me.

DUKE SOLINUS
Speak freely, Syracusian, what thou wilt.

AEGEON
Is not your name, sir, call'd Antipholus?
And is not that your bondman, Dromio?

DROMIO OF EPHESUS
Within this hour I was his bondman sir,
But he, I thank him, gnaw'd in two my cords:
Now am I Dromio and his man unbound.

AEGEON
I am sure you both of you remember me.

DROMIO OF EPHESUS
Ourselves we do remember, sir, by you;
For lately we were bound, as you are now
You are not Pinch's patient, are you, sir?

AEGEON
Why look you strange on me? you know me well.

ANTIPHOLUS
I never saw you in my life till now.

AEGEON
O, grief hath changed me since you saw me last,
And careful hours with time's deformed hand
Have written strange defeatures in my face:
But tell me yet, dost thou not know my voice?

ANTIPHOLUS OF EPHESUS
Neither.

AEGEON
Dromio, nor thou?

DROMIO OF EPHESUS
No, trust me, sir, nor I.

AEGEON
I am sure thou dost.

DROMIO OF EPHESUS
Ay, sir, but I am sure I do not; and whatsoever a
man denies, you are now bound to believe him.

AEGEON
Not know my voice! O time's extremity,
Hast thou so crack'd and splitted my poor tongue
In seven short years, that here my only son
Knows not my feeble key of untuned cares?
Though now this grained face of mine be hid
In sap-consuming winter's drizzled snow,
And all the conduits of my blood froze up,
Yet hath my night of life some memory,
My wasting lamps some fading glimmer left,
My dull deaf ears a little use to hear:

All these old witnesses--I cannot err--
Tell me thou art my son Antipholus.

ANTIPHOLUS OF EPHESUS
I never saw my father in my life.

AEGEON
But seven years since, in Syracusa, boy,
Thou know'st we parted: but perhaps, my son,
Thou shamest to acknowledge me in misery.

ANTIPHOLUS OF EPHESUS
The duke and all that know me in the city
Can witness with me that it is not so
I ne'er saw Syracusa in my life.

DUKE SOLINUS
I tell thee, Syracusian, twenty years
Have I been patron to Antipholus,
During which time he ne'er saw Syracusa:
I see thy age and dangers make thee dote.

Re-enter AEMILIA, with ANTIPHOLUS of Syracuse and
DROMIO of Syracuse

AEMELIA
Most mighty duke, behold a man much wrong'd.

All gather to see them

ADRIANA
I see two husbands, or mine eyes deceive me.

DUKE SOLINUS
One of these men is Genius to the other;
And so of these. Which is the natural man,
And which the spirit? who deciphers them?

DROMIO OF SYRACUSE
I, sir, am Dromio; command him away.

DROMIO OF EPHESUS
I, sir, am Dromio; pray, let me stay.

ANTIPHOLUS OF SYRACUSE
AEgeon art thou not? or else his ghost?

DROMIO OF SYRACUSE
O, my old master! who hath bound him here?

AEMELIA
Whoever bound him, I will loose his bonds
And gain a husband by his liberty.
Speak, old AEgeon, if thou be'st the man
That hadst a wife once call'd AEmilia
That bore thee at a burden two fair sons:
O, if thou be'st the same AEgeon, speak,
And speak unto the same AEmilia!

AEGEON
If I dream not, thou art AEmilia:
If thou art she, tell me where is that son
That floated with thee on the fatal raft?

AEMELIA
By men of Epidamnum he and I
And the twin Dromio all were taken up;
But by and by rude fishermen of Corinth
By force took Dromio and my son from them
And me they left with those of Epidamnum.
What then became of them I cannot tell
I to this fortune that you see me in.

DUKE SOLINUS
Why, here begins his morning story right;
These two Antipholuses, these two so like,
And these two Dromios, one in semblance,--

Besides her urging of her wreck at sea,--
These are the parents to these children,
Which accidentally are met together.
Antipholus, thou camest from Corinth first?

ANTIPHOLUS OF SYRACUSE
No, sir, not I; I came from Syracuse.

DUKE SOLINUS
Stay, stand apart; I know not which is which.

ANTIPHOLUS OF EPHESUS
I came from Corinth, my most gracious lord,--

DROMIO OF EPHESUS
And I with him.

ANTIPHOLUS OF EPHESUS
Brought to this town by that most famous warrior,
Duke Menaphon, your most renowned uncle.

ADRIANA
Which of you two did dine with me to-day?

ANTIPHOLUS OF SYRACUSE
I, gentle mistress.

ADRIANA
And are not you my husband?

ANTIPHOLUS OF EPHESUS
No; I say nay to that.

ANTIPHOLUS OF SYRACUSE
And so do I; yet did she call me so:
And this fair gentlewoman, her sister here,
Did call me brother.

To Luciana

What I told you then,
I hope I shall have leisure to make good;
If this be not a dream I see and hear.

ANGELO
That is the chain, sir, which you had of me.

ANTIPHOLUS OF SYRACUSE
I think it be, sir; I deny it not.

ANTIPHOLUS OF EPHESUS
And you, sir, for this chain arrested me.

ANGELO
I think I did, sir; I deny it not.

ADRIANA
I sent you money, sir, to be your bail,
By Dromio; but I think he brought it not.

DROMIO OF EPHESUS
No, none by me.

ANTIPHOLUS OF SYRACUSE
This purse of ducats I received from you,
And Dromio, my man, did bring them me.
I see we still did meet each other's man,
And I was ta'en for him, and he for me,
And thereupon these errors are arose.

ANTIPHOLUS OF EPHESUS
These ducats pawn I for my father here.

DUKE SOLINUS
It shall not need; thy father hath his life.

Courtezan
Sir, I must have that diamond from you.

ANTIPHOLUS OF EPHESUS
There, take it; and much thanks for my good cheer.

AEMELIA
Renowned duke, vouchsafe to take the pains
To go with us into the abbey here
And hear at large discoursed all our fortunes:
And all that are assembled in this place,
That by this sympathized one day's error
Have suffer'd wrong, go keep us company,
And we shall make full satisfaction.
Thirty-three years have I but gone in travail
Of you, my sons; and till this present hour
My heavy burden ne'er delivered.
The duke, my husband and my children both,
And you the calendars of their nativity,
Go to a gossips' feast and go with me;
After so long grief, such festivity!

DUKE SOLINUS
With all my heart, I'll gossip at this feast.

Exeunt all but Antipholus of Syracuse, Antipholus of
Ephesus, Dromio of Syracuse and Dromio of Ephesus

DROMIO OF SYRACUSE
Master, shall I fetch your stuff from shipboard?

ANTIPHOLUS OF EPHESUS
Dromio, what stuff of mine hast thou embark'd?

DROMIO OF SYRACUSE
Your goods that lay at host, sir, in the Centaur.

ANTIPHOLUS OF SYRACUSE
He speaks to me. I am your master, Dromio:

Come, go with us; we'll look to that anon:
Embrace thy brother there; rejoice with him.

Exeunt Antipholus of Syracuse and Antipholus of
Ephesus

DROMIO OF SYRACUSE
There is a fat friend at your master's house,
That kitchen'd me for you to-day at dinner:
She now shall be my sister, not my wife.

DROMIO OF EPHESUS
Methinks you are my glass, and not my brother:
I see by you I am a sweet-faced youth.
Will you walk in to see their gossiping?

DROMIO OF SYRACUSE
Not I, sir; you are my elder.

DROMIO OF EPHESUS
That's a question: how shall we try it?

DROMIO OF SYRACUSE
We'll draw cuts for the senior: till then lead thou first.

DROMIO OF EPHESUS
Nay, then, thus:
We came into the world like brother and brother;
And now let's go hand in hand, not one before
another.

Exeunt

CPSIA information can be obtained
at www.ICGtesting.com
Printed in the USA
LVOW12s1608220916
505792LV00002B/300/P